s l a k e

To Emma,
one of the sweetest, kindest,
most beautiful (inside and
out) friends I've ever had.
I'll miss you at school! Love
you and praying for you!
Maggie Rothrock

slake

a journey in po

-etry

by margaret j. rothrock

keysandthings publications
wheaton, illinois

Printed in the United States of America

First printing 2017

ISBN 978-1548372200

KeysandThings Publications
CPO 2408
501 College Ave
Wheaton, IL 60187

www.keysandthings.blog

How precious is your steadfast love, O God!
The children of mankind take refuge in the
shadow of your wings.
They feast on the abundance of your house,
and you give them drink from the river of
your delights.
For with you is the fountain of life;
in your light do we see light.

Psalm 36:7-9

contents

II   crossing

III   the promised land

V   the new earth

a note

sip poetry with lemonade,
drink it in and feel it slipping coolly
down your throat
into your chest to calm
your heartbeat and lull it
into the rhythm of the universe.

sip poetry with spiced herbal tea
and stir it with a spoon to
make the sugar dissolve
and slake your thirst with sweetness
and sourness
and spiciness
and everything you needed,
with everythingness.

sip poetry or gulp it
quench your image-hungry thirst
taste the variance of flavors and colors
and let them wash for a moment through your chest:
translucent concoctions of
squeezed lemons or crushed leaves:
for poetry
is extracted from experience
and must be drunk.

I

the wilderness

Miles and Miles

can you hear the way the
rain rushes across the
roof tiles?

the green grass is glowing
and the restive rain rushing
miles and miles

down the farmlands, the
valleys, and everything we
didn't want wet.

it's so dark, it's so
grey, so much rain and clouds. we
wanted to forget

how everything could be so cold,
so full of emptiness
rushing.

but the rain
keeps gushing.

Ending, All Ending

There's not enough Time
(Watch, it brings all its dusts
Out to cover the floor,
Simmers slowly and rusts
All the pipes, and the door
Gets a cringe-worthy squeak
In its hinges, and groans
At the bones of the week
Passing by).

There's not enough Time
(Still we set it up nice,
All the tables made straight
And the settings checked twice,
But I don't know the reason
When after a blink
We'll be done and move on
And cease ever to think of
Today).

There's not enough Time
(Here's the table for two,
All the dishes, they gleam
As if everything's new,
But the cracks will appear
Before we can enjoy them
And try as we might
We can't flee from the ploy
Prone to fly).

There's not enough Time
(Look, the sun's going down,
And our candles are burnt
To a charred ghoulish frown,
So you'd think we'd have learnt.
Underneath this old sun
Dinner's ending, all ending—
We've no shot but one on
This earth).

Shooting No. 7,388,562

It's Cain—it's Cain
    all over again—
        only, this time his arms are
        of steel.
And damming that bloodflow is even less hard
    when his fingers
    don't have to
    feel.

Everyone's
Able to fall in a field, unhappy and
    lacking renown;
And those yet honored
    are nonetheless dead. (You can find them, a
        long
        long
        way down.)
And while Cain keeps killing, we
    can't bring them back.
A curse of a power
        we own!
To spill and to slaughter,
    dig blood-rivers broader
        than ever.
            —Yet never
Atone.

Inevitable

the train is coming
coming coming
hurtles down the tracks and
hits obstructions
never yields it is
utterly
inevit
-able

it never stops
it never waits
it never slows or
hesitates it's
not about to stop no it's
inev
-itable

the train is coming
watch it looms
it dogs our steps
it blocks our hopes
there's no more room,
it runs us down, we

can't escape
we can't escape
we watch it rush
we watch it crush yet

watching it won't buy us time, still
coming coming
coming, our death is.

And Another One Down

I can do nothing, nothing at all.
Nothing
nada
zilch
at all.
The world has fallen apart since the Fall;
and I can do nothing,
nothing at all.

Can *I* do something to
change this mess? Can *I*
be impetus for less
of blood and less
of hate at all?
The world continues to cry
and crawl—

the blood clots up, it spills, it dries—
it streams and falls; please, close your eyes;
there's no point looking when nothing at all
can fix the spilling,
can fix
the Fall.

On the World Spins—I Mean the Laundry

Laundry again
yes: a cycle of ten
inconveniences. Let me explain:
the first is I do it with
nothing to show, yet I do it. My weekly refrain.

The second involves how the socks leave their loves
and the third, that they never regain
their partners again once
they've split themselves up.
The fourth, divorced socks
feel vain.

The fifth is how dim
all the whites will become
on the fiftieth washing. (You'll see.)
The sixth is how trim
all the shirts used to be
but now need to be starched. I'm not free.

And seventh, the sweaters keep
aging and shrinking: I swear they'll never stop.
And eighth, all the stains from the dishrags I used
have left blood on the white of my top.

Ninth, blood provides
such a sticking red stain.
Its permanence ever will deign
to jive at the tenth thing:
again and again
I do laundry & life.
My refrain.

One of Those Days

Like trudging through half-dried concrete mix,
this day is.
There is nothing and no one to
ease the work, and I only hope someone
will help me find the path of least resistance.

Like digging through solid rock,
this day is.
My pickaxe and shovel can hardly
make a dent on the cave wall,
but I've got to; simply must.

Frustrating,
this day is.
So much to do.
So little time to do it.
Frustrating.
The only thing that keeps me going is that
maybe tomorrow,
when I've broken through the wall,
there'll be clean, open air.

Ensconcement

One knows what it is like
        to frequent a cocoon,
        grey wool around the face
        with a small backwards-telescope hole for the eyes.
Small and stingy,
        wrapped in oneself,
        unattractive
        and uncaring.
One says one is only tired,
        but it is really the thought of addressing another in
        the Second Person that
        drains;
The thought of creating something one has
        already created a thousand times, of
        upholding something unworthy to be upheld,
        of sustaining a love that
        like all life
        is bound to die in a year or so.
This thought is what keeps one
        tucked in melancholic folds
        though life spins around sunnily.
It seems, if there were a name for such ensconcement,
        it would best be "silken
        shroud."

This is Not a Circle

I crave completion; only that;
a better place, a fuller world,
    alignment of the midnight sky so all the stars
      can show us where
         we're meant to go
        and what we'll find
           in other air—

    but clouds are clotting up the light,
        the constellations gleam but dim;
  reflecting this, my respiratory system, on a whim,
      begins to wheeze, though silently—
        the rasp of partial breaths soon gone—
              and violently they
          take from me the chance
       to circle on and on—

friend, say you've felt it too! oh you can feel
    the rasping through my skin:
        you've felt it through yourself straight from
        my hesitating heartbeat, in
  the uncontinued circle, through the stars
        and through our touch:
        you feel the rasping; say you do:
  or else—

           I am alone—

but—
—oh, it doesn't matter much.

you feel it, don't you?
do you? don't?
I s'pose I'll never know.
I'd have to ask you outright, loud
for you to say it's so,
and I could never ask, in case
you wouldn't understand;
I've seen uncircles circling
comprehension, firsthand.

and, I'm *used* to finding holes in stars, and know,
perhaps you're not. I can't ask, for lungs like mine
breathe harder than they ought;

I live in imperfection: see,

—but this is hardly new,
I crave—you know, I really do—
a world washed clean of broken rhymes
and broken stars—
and broken—

me—

Mirror

I am the reflection in the mirror,
the image of him who formed me from the earth.
I love his land of wonder, and the beauty in his eyes;
there is nothing I despise; for he supplies.
And yet.
And yet—

it beckons me, what cannot be—
no, must not be, he says, or I will die:
it beckons me, what must not be,
the knowledge that I cannot,
while I'm in the mirror,
see.
The Knowledge from the Tree.

"Ah, knowledge will not *kill* you," hisses
something in my ear.
"To leave this flat dimension for
the round one knowledge brings
is not to die," it whispers—faintly, but
I hear.
"Indeed, by breaking from Obedience,
you'll know the secrets of this cryptic world," it says to me.
"Why, just as *he* is free, so *you* will be."

I think of how he moves, and sees, and knows—
while I'm imprisoned, everywhere he goes,
he sees.
He—alone—is free.
Let *me*, I think. Let me as well be free.

And so,
my mind made up,
my fingers follow what is surely good—they
reach. I
touch. I
push.

Cracks, a spider's web, weave out from where I placed the
impact,   making lace
of solid glass,
and as my fingers frac
                    ture the perfection of my past,
I feel something I have never felt inside the mirror:
the double-
        bladed
shards
                piercing
        skin.

Tearing in,
        the sting of sin   propels my tearing out. I
                                            fall
                through broken glass
    in blood   in pain   a curse in me;
                            and finally unbound, I meet
    the ground   the shards   my misery.
Now I know.
Now I see,
        everything
        that matters in the world:
                for I and the mirror are one, and,
                        as one,

                    we have shattered.

What Used to Be a Soul

Shaky breaths in.
Her chest trembles and her hand does, too,
as she reaches into the ashes
for what used to be her heart.

There isn't much left, now;
the smooth bit might have been the bit that once
loved, only it's worn from overuse.
The rough bit is likely the callused part
that hardened over all the tenderness
she used to have.
The cracked white-ash bit is
her future, she is
almost sure, her eternity all up in flames;
and there is nothing else, no other meaning
in this lump that used to be a heart.

Perhaps she is mad to grab a still-hot coal
from the fireplace and gaze at it in this way,
but the coal was once a living tree, and her heart
was once living flesh, and the metaphor
is not too far from the truth.
Why does fire consume so completely?
Why is life a fire that burns and burns
until her heart no longer beats
and her future is no longer a future but
a bit of cracked white ash
on a dry, dead piece of wood?

She has loved, and she has been loved.
She has hurt, and she has been hurt.
And now there is nothing left
but the cinder-girl, with her shaky breaths,
staring at this piece of still-hot coal,
and her heart's similar fate.

All she can do is mourn
what used to be a soul.

Pride

Accidentally
She touched the lowest brick on the tower
And it fell.

To You (Me)

Fear,
    O you who cannot Live, for
    from Pandora's box you have released
    your own unfathomed agony.
Abhor
    the light which flickers
    on your blinded eyes,
    revealing sins and ruins, your debris.
Lament
    your wretched state, and all the
    righteousness you lost;
Learn
    to live with every scar
    you bought, at such a cost;
Envy
    perfect angels, who have
    never felt this burn; and
Numb
    the pain and dull the sword,
    and maybe you'll survive (for now)
    with what you've justly earned.

Denial

i won't
i won't i won't i won't i
won't i WILL NOT no no no
don't make me, stop geroff me i don't want
your hands all over me no i don't need help because
i don't need to go anywhere, i am NOT stuck
in a pit and i do NOT need
a ladder and i MOST CERTAINLY do not need
anyone to lift me out
because i'm not leaving, i like it here
(ok it's a little dark yeah but
well i well i like the dark)
get away stop saying you're trying to
rescue me you're not i like it here better than there
that's not rescuing if i like it here better than there
i don't need a shower it's better in the dirt
(ok it smells a little funny but
well i well i like the smell)
no no no i won't no
stop saying you're trying to help me it
isn't helping anything you're wrong you're wrong
i don't care about germs i don't care about
eating i don't care about light
i like it here i don't care if the cockroaches make me sick
(ok i care kinda but)
I WILL NOT do what you tell me to do
because (even though ok you're maybe kinda right)
this is MY pit this is MY way and
Daddy you ain't the boss of me.

Immured

Immured in the walls of myself, I hide
And there my silent thoughts abide
All buried deep so none can see
The Truth of Who is really Me.

Hindenburg

I'm a balloon and I
Soak up sin.
My valves open up and
They let it all in.
It weighs on me, works me, it wrenches me down:
It catches on fire and makes me to drown
In the flames, in the flames of the hydrogen
Bomb:

I've inflated with folly—
And will die by its arm.

Tiger

A tiger lies dormant
in my chest,
curled fetally—stored
energy that waits for any reason to
send it scratching my
ribcage-battlements,
to tear out my heart and my lungs
and escape to do the same to those of
other men—

but perhaps it does not lie dormant;
perhaps dormant is
too passive a
word, it drags against my inward parts—
I can feel its breath—the
pressure and release and
pressure and release and
pressure and release as
it awaits the moment
of revelation—the moment of
devastation—

the moment when
I am discovered and my sins
spill forth—

Sweet Venom

Cupid
Doesn't shoot his arrows,
You
Do.
Every time you say my name
You send a shiver down my frame
And start the piercing, painful game
Of aiming poison straight
And sure
And true.

Sometimes arrows shoot
Into my fingers,
Giving them desire to cling to yours.

Sometimes arrows root
Inside my gaze, and then it lingers,
Bloodied with the longing arrow-sores.

A prick, a point,
It isn't much;
A tiny dose,
A single touch;
But love and poison shouldn't flow
Together in my veins, you know,
And as they always, always do,
How can I help but think of you?

Madness from You

There was you and there was me—
Just us, together only three;
And your stare was in my brain
As was your tangled lion's mane,
And there was nothing much beside—
My wits are gone, long's you abide;
Perhaps I'll peek beneath
The chair; but no, there's
No use looking there;
Your stare!
That's where I'll find my scattered mind
And lose it all again and grind my
One two three five wits
To bits
Of lint upon the breeze.

I Know I Know I Broke It

Let's not mention what I should have known;
       I was wrong, okay? I was wrong.
             I thought I could find the truth on my own
But I know
—yes, I know—

                          I was wrong.
      I'm only a girl with a half of a brain
       And I thought it was whole, smart and strong.
But really I thought far too much of myself.
Now I know: I was wrong all along.

Undefined Terms

Does zero fit in one a thousand times or none at all?
And do the waves grow bigger if a hundred raindrops
    fall?
Can any human swim across ten oceans and a sea?
And was your love for one a chain from which you've
    broken free?

Can any million lovers fill the hole inside my heart?
If so then will the million pieces simply fall apart?
With glue and memories forgot perhaps they'll stay intact,
But maybe they will never heal. Without you, I've
Cracked.

Scrambled Shards

Life is such a scramble,
such an unforgiving
mess.
We love these
shar ds of bro k en glass
and hope they've
righteousness.
I think—it used to be—a vase—
but it's so hard to see,
my own glass pieces fall on his
and who is whole?
Him or me?

The Mirror-World

Reflections are everywhere, all around us.
Your gaze reflects in the polished bronze candlesticks
and the flames of the candles
are kindled in your eyes,
and the dark windows throw back
our impassioned silhouettes
and show us ourselves—
and our lies.

I see in the mirror-world that
hands I thought I held are mirages,
and you cringe when my fingers come near.
I see in the mirror-world that
lips I thought I kissed are not so round or soft
or welcoming, but rather
pursed; truly,
I see in the mirror-world,
they leer.

Reflections are everywhere, all around us.
In the mirror-world I see that
things are not as they seem,   and seem not as they are.
That purses are tight   and tight too are your lips
—and I, a lowly mortal, cannot hope to come into either.
That the brightest star
may also be the smallest
though it beckons in the night.

Reflections are everywhere, all around us.
They see;   see, they
are flickering in your face and in the candles.
Are simmering in the dark windowpanes
and reminding us of everything
we thought we could ignore.
And what did we think that for?
All around us, though we look for other ways to look,
our self-deceptions stare us down.
Everywhere are reflections.

October

It really is October:
and leaves so often sober
drink a little bit too much, and all
the giddy, gaudy colors swirling down
disguise a touch of something
pressing, some old foe;
a tipsy, bitter woe—
for autumn winds are alcohol to drown
the thought of snow.

I see your hesitation:
and in the fragmentation I see
all you do to lose yourself
in swirling leaves; the memories,
behind a ruse of joy, hide
in the wind's exhale,
an ice-clear veil:
for things you thought you could forget
have made you frail.

It really is October.
And everything is sober underneath
the autumn craze and now
the fragrance of the outward act
is covering a haze of something
putrid, something old:
a contrast with the bold
and busy colors of your laugh:
there lies the cold.

Ariadne

Ariadne, standing by the door,
Looks long into the empty labyrinth.

Whispers of the memories within
Come coiling snakelike round her trembling heart
And squeeze it till it quiets and barely beats.
So have his arms encircled round her, like the wall
That keeps the castle safe from harm;
So strong, so firm, no shadow of the way
His promises would fall as snakeskins fall,
As so many lives have fallen in the maze.
At least the Minotaur devours no more.
The hero they called devout took care of that.

For, men marvel at his piety,
His love for country, family, for gods
And men—and Theseus has battled well
Against the enemies of all of these.
And, Ariadne marveled at him too;
And still she tries to think of him as good,
Ignoring all the turmoil in her mind.
But why she tries to think of him that way
She couldn't tell. For truth hints otherwise.
The loyal Theseus has left her here,
And deep inside she knows he'll not be back.

Ariadne, standing by the door,
Remembers. Now the ravaged maze is bare—
And too her ravaged arms. There's only air.

Tracing

In sharp relief, three rows ahead of me,
A profile I can never touch. I trace
The lines in undiluted lunacy,
Reviving the perfections of the face;
The eyes, the lips, the furrow of the brow
Inscribed upon my vision from years past,
But singed into my marrow, scarring now,
A lasting mark of love that didn't last.
I once was seated cherished on a throne,
Attended by your tender, caring show;
And now, I sit and trace you, all alone
With visions I'm ashamed for you to know.
       It's hard to blame you, even for such a theft;
       I still trace broken thrones, although you left.

Bye-Bye Balloons

I'm chasing the wind—
                                              ()
                                              /*

                              I can taste it—a bit—
SSSSSSSS

        at times, I catch up, and—

                      SSSSSSSSS< touch, and—

                                          SSSSSS   ()
                              .   SSSSS   /*
                          . 1 -   /

                      .
                      .l.

well, that's it.

Arm Yourself

Arm yourself:
Take up the hard-hearted shield,
And the glass weapons that are tears
Can be fended off.

Enemies will come:
But you must not succumb
To Emotion. Who needs
Emotion?
It may cut into your heart.
(That is what the shield
Is for.)

They need never know:
Scorn, they will.
Attack, they shall.
Enemies always do,
When you are feeling at your
Lowest.

But you can fight:
You're not a baby, you're not
Susceptible. Hold your shield
Proudly. Plug your ears.
You can pretend
Not to care.

Tables Turned

Give me your hand.
I'll take it, as I take your proffered love,
And read the lines in your palm
As coldly, as stiffly, and
With as much disinterest
As you used to have in me.
You see, I'm immune now.

Give me your trust.
Give it as I gave you mine,
Before I was desirable,
Before I was beautiful,
Before you ever thought of wanting me;
And after you do,
I'll betray it a thousand times—
For I'm not cruel enough to pay you back in full.

Give me your heart.
No doubt it will hurt,
When I squeeze it,
And especially when I return it
In pieces.
But that's what I'll do,
As you did to me,
Only I'll revel in your pain
Instead of ignoring it.

I already gave you my all;
I owe you nothing,
Now that you give *your* all
To me.

She Plays

She plays
until her arms hurt,
she plays
until her wrists won't move,
she plays
until her fingers stop
and refuse to hit one more key.

She stays
until her head hurts,
she stays
until her body aches,
she stays
until her back shoots pain
up her spine and down her limbs.

And the more she plays,
the less she can do,
and the fewer notes she hits,
and the harder everything becomes.

Her fingers feel shaky like gelatin
shaking and imprecise on the serving dish,
they fall
on the keys
randomly.

So why does she keep at it?

Now that's the question,
isn't it?

...And She Plays

Some escape by fun.
Some by work.
Some by ease.
I escape by pounding on
The gleaming ivories.

Not so lonely now my fingers
Stretch and crawl and glide.
Not so lonely hearing all the triads coincide.

Some escape by rants.
Some by shouts.
Some by pleas.
I escape by singing, scaling, screaming
On the keys.

Bitter? Oh, Not at All

Say, what a pleasure it is to be sick.
Of all of the pleasures, the one I would pick.
You lie with a pile of cough drops in bed
Ignoring the pounding inside of your head,
And listen to everyone getting things done
And look at your task list, accomplishing none,
And balk as the teachers explain what you've missed:

It's pleasure, at least, when you're burning the list
With your fever. (It catches on fire, it does.)

The arson inside me is full of warm fuzz.

A Lament for Modern Poetry

Your words, I fear, they just
don't make sense to us commonfolk
who want our wares wrapped in
clean white ribbons—tell me,
why
does the age of emojis
bring with it the age of poetic abstraction?
(Perhaps we must spew our
melancholy somewhere,
outside of the realm of loling?)
Truly, I can do this too,
speak of memories lost to mists of time and
the whispers of the dead and
I can end
on a line without a period

—as can anyone
—tell me,
what is it that makes the mention of a moon
transform discrete and unoriginal images into
magic
in your mind?

What is it that offends the ear
when symphonies are woven
into paper poetry?
Rhyme and rhythm and reason
have no place
on a page anymore

.

Calc Smash Smash

I haven't written anything
In ohsovery long;
My words just won't conform themselves
To poetry or song;
I'm dry of metaphors, just as
I'm broke of extra cash,
And math has hammered flat my rhymes—
CALC
SMASH
smash.

Two Hundred Poems Later

I fear all the time that I'm losing
my touch. If writing comes
easy, it's harder to clutch at
its worth and remember
the syllables sound
in the same way they did.
(Built in bricks from the ground.)

For what if I'm worser at words
than before, and what if my grammar
is suddenly poor, and
what if my symbols are dullened and dead
and procrastination has
lifted his head?

I feel like I'm falling in
patterns of thought, writing everything over again
that I've got and I don't know if That makes me better
or worse.
If a clearer day's dawned or
has opened my hearse.

So I write and I write.
And I play and I play.
And I pray and I pray that my talents will stay
so that someday I'll find something
better than great.
No fish rotting on last year's plate.

Ecclesiastes Hourglass

if you sit still   you can feel the seconds   sliding by.
time's roller blades are silent   but you know they're there, for
the guards chisel wrinkles   in your face, and   the wheels' rotations'
heartbeats will run out eventually,
                                        we're all well aware.

you may not hear the sand   slipping down   through the hourglass,
but that little transparent passage is   the only thing   between
You and   The End.   you know because   the   white
sand is cascading   onto your head and   dyeing your hair to match.
truth.

grasp   at it as you will, but   time is   fluid   and
you can't   catch an ocean mist any more
than you can pin a bubble to your
                        bulletin board and immortalize it
for your children's grandchildren
                in 3026 a.d. since an ocean mist
        is more solid than memories
                and much more predictable
                                than time.

what are we,then,and What Is Life if we are all
just waiting for the roller   blades to dig
their heels in and   halt? even the white
hairs won't come with you to the grave,not that you're
        aware of, anyway, for
you'll be drowned   in ocean mists   by then.
history is supposed to leave a mark   but does it really?
the greeks are dead and the romans are
        dead and the egyptians are dead and

all we have left are the remnants
        of the soap bubbles with the pinholes in them.
                pop goes the civilization.
vapor of vapors! under a   sun like ours you'll find you've no
control over time except there are ways   to stop the skates
faster, ways to lose   the mists to the running sand-timer current,
ways to hasten   the greying of your hair.
                        truth.

so maybe we should   stop clutching at time and look
above   the sun instead?

The Princess Who Lost Eden

Snow White had,
   always, been sweet;
   her blackberry hair,
   and cherry cheeks,
   just added to her
      pomegranate smile,
   and,
      once in a while,
   she'd burst into laughter
   for no real reason
   at all;
   besides—
   perhaps—
   a gratitude for
   Love, and all the things
   it had to give.
In short,
   perfection
      was her soul,
      and good
   her predilection.

But followed by
        misfortune,
   the sugar-coat around her life
   soon
s p l i n t e r e
                  d
   as the second-fairest serpent

(oops, a queen, not serpentine)
besought
      REVENGE.

For SPITE
  was *her* cup of tea,
and once the looking-glass
    had ceased to lie, she,
      in awful temper, crept,
      stepped into the Garden—
            rose to strike—
      an apple in her scaly hand,
                and filled
                with POISON—

    But I am ahead of myself.

Snow White,
      meantime,
          found seven
             small
             men,
                worked their garden cheerily awhile,
                wondered at the very beautiful
                   redness
                of the apples they told her not to eat
                on the tree,

and
  discovered that a scheme had been devised.
        Though in her heart she never
      recognized the danger to
          her soul.

No worry overcame her,
        just assurance that she could,
with ease,
        withstand
whatever
                the Deceiver
had to offer.

                                And NOW shall enter

        the Snake—
        no, the queen—
with her, the
glossy apple, red as blood—
    and a hunger
            for the rider of the pale horse.
                            (Death.)

Snow White
    comes out;
    and all at once her
                perfect heart
    is nibbled by Desire.
The apple,
    the blood-red apple;
the sheen of power,
    spread across its shining scarlet skin;

and temptation
has ruined her.

She bites.

She falls.

And with her, humanity.

This is the Death of Snow White.

She will rest

until

her Prince arrives.

Man of Sorrows

she came to him, greatly changed:
if it had not been so long, I would have
placed the difference better, but perhaps
it hung in the limp look of her eyes or the marks
(scabs and scars) on her skin, or perhaps
it was the slight hunch in her shoulders, the smallness
of the way she held herself;
anyhow,

she came to him, crumpled, and crumbling at his feet
clung to the last of her possessions for a moment,
a half-eaten apple turned brown and covered in mold
so much like the one I, too, held;
then she threw it before him
in utter submission, a vessel of despair.

You're back, he said, after so long.
She said nothing, eyes on the fruit she had
so desperately thrown away, and maybe
she saw the tips of his feet, too, the bareness
and the calluses and the dirt,
as he stepped toward her
and placed his hand on her shoulder:

two entities one in
mourning, and yet one also in peace:

I came upon them in this way, a single figure
of sorrows.

He pulled two things from his satchel,
first, a loaf of bread that had not been allowed to rise,
then a cup which he filled from the flask at his side
with a deep red liquid, like blood. She took them
and I noticed the pungent fragrance from the cup,
the smell of wine
that covered the sick sweetness of the rotten apples.
She noticed too, and at last
gazed at his face.

I must give up everything?—she asked.
I am giving up everything, he said.
I know, she said. And I must too.
And she ate.
And she drank.

I watched them, silent,
and wondered what it meant to be free
of rot. To let go of sourness. To drench myself
in a fountain of cleanness and quench my thirst
with the sorrow-man's wine.

Three
steps
I took towards him.

He looked at me, with eyes as clear as jewels,
eyes that loved, but eyes, too, that
stabbed.
Are you ready to give it all up? He asked,
gravely, tenderly; I love you.

I squeezed the apple in my hand,
let the rotten smell come into my nostrils, and
looked away from him, for his gaze cut me;
I can't give anything to this man, I thought.
He knows me too well.

And I turned, and I ran away.

A week later I heard he was dead.

All I had done in his life
was add to his rejections.
He offered me life, and I
added to him
sorrow.

Crime and Punishment

I killed an innocent man.
I let the murderer go free
And in his place upon the tree
I nailed and stabbed an innocent man.
And I don't really understand.

I killed an innocent man.
Why'd I do it? Why, when he
Deserved to live eternally,
And here, I killed him, wittingly?
And let the murderer go free.

I killed an innocent man.
His blood is spattered over me,
Because I nailed him to the tree,
Because I killed him, wittingly,
And death came just as I had planned.

I killed an innocent man.
I killed him, tortured him, you see
I watched his blood flow vilely,
I watched him cry, I heard his plea,
I let the murderer go free—

He let the murderer go free—

Because I killed him there—and yet—
And I don't really understand—
He died for
Me.

The Fall of Jerusalem

the rain rain rain
gushing rushing flushing sweeps away the
sinking sand
and leaves the house to
crumble.

the pain pain pain
as it gushes rushes flushes pounding
hard
upon the wounds
hard
upon the skin
upon the
hard
heart.

the gain gain gain
what gain? there's none:
the house has
fallen and the shaky ground has
shaken
and i've watched my walls careening to the
quaking
earth.
and there i'm fixed in ruin and in ruins
lying crying dying
cannot sleep or wake
but all the rain hurts
far
too much to be a
dream.

on and on and on it pounds
it pounds; it pounds
it wounds—
in dreams
rain does not wound. so
i'm awake, in misery,
in lifeless breath,
in quickest death,
i'm dying for the pain but
living
still.

still i lie
still i
gushing rushing flushing
hurt
still i
on and on and on
it pounds,
the cleansing river
that has scourged
and washed away my world.

Takeoff

It throbs,
It pounds:
Tha THUMP tha THUMP
My head
In time with my
Heartbeat.
The voice
Resounds
Just JUMP just JUMP
Instead
Of standing on
Concrete.
Your feet
Are firm,
But where's your heart?
It rages
Wild as the
Ocean.
Know, it
Will calm,
Its peace will start,
When you
Trade safety
For motion.
My head—
It hurts—
Tha THUMP tha THUMP
Just go,
It tells me,
Just go.
I've wavered,
Waffled:

Paralyzed:
But deep inside
I know.
I have
To give
This faith
A chance.
I have to be brave
And fly.
I steel my nerves.
Take a backward glance.
And run
Into the sky.

So now
I've made
My choice—
My choice,
Between
The sky and fear;
The throbbing
Stops.
The pounding
Drops.
We'll see where I fly
From here.

Saturday

A banner in a bright parade,
A victor with a silver blade,
A leader she'd believed, obeyed.

And there he was inside the tomb:
An empty, cold, unchanging room
For someone supposed to conquer doom.

And she was left outside alone
And in her heart there lay a stone
As in the tomb there lay his throne.

Dead and Dead

He's dead.
He's dead.
He's deader than deader than dead.

The eyes that used to watch me dead.
The arms that used to hold me dead.
The heart that used to love me dead.
The strength I thought would save me, fled.

The ears that used to listen dead.
The mind that used to reason dead.
The hands that used to heal, dead
And stiff and cold as lead.

Of cold dark stone they made his bed,
On linen cloth they laid his head;
I thought he was the Christ, he said.
And now his cross drips red.
He's dead.

See You Again?

how could he be dead?
i cast my waiting hopes on him,
i learned to fish, i learned to swim,
i learned to dive and cleanse and slake
inside his peace, inside his lake,
and here he is inside a tomb.
my savior, stone and cold, entombed.

the living waters—but, he said
he had them—they were his—and yet
he's lying underneath the ground,
in dried-up blood and water, dead,
the living waters left him as he bled?

i loved him and he lived, i thought,
i thought he lived in me, and now my love
is all for naught, is all for naught,
is all for naught.

that is, if he's not able—
a man born in a stable to a virgin's more than man—
if i can trust—but who can conquer death?
—if i can trust instead that he is able—
can a corpse
rise from the dead?

II

crossing

One Moment

In an instant
            everything can change.

A woman crumpled up in agony
can utter out a groan of pain and from
a writing womb welcome a child which moves,
which breathes, which *lives,*
            though it comes from nothingness:

and

      a body in a grave, swaddled in clothes
so like the newborn's, but in eternal rest
instead of in the dawning of a life,

can waken from that sleep.

We longed, we yearned for something more than earth,

more than cycles,
            the way the world revolved,
the endless seasons, sicknesses, and strains,
the heartache and the thousand natural shocks
that flesh is heir to—

than thirst,
            the thirst for something deeper, clearer
than the tainted waters we received on earth—

than endings—
                hate—
                        bloodshed—
                                pain—
                                        and death—

But now!—
                One instant can make everything
                                change.

Watch, the newborn leaves its mother's womb:

and

        the dead man folds his wrinkled linen clothes,
and walks from the tomb.

                        This dead man is alive—
see, the stone rolls back, and the doors of death
                                fling wide—
and there—there's life, I see eternity—
there's after all a purpose in the midst
of all the cycles—our brokenness is healed—
our hope, finally infinite and sure—

an instant, and a tomb is rearranged:
and now God's left the grave,
                        the whole world's
                        changed.

III

the promised land

Pulse

Three fingers
against her wrist.

Two seconds
silence—
then—

One heart,
beating.

ALIVE ALIVE

He's alive He's alive!,—
                ring bells, climb church towers and
                      strike hand bells against the church
                          bells as they ring and
          yell (oh goodness YELL with your whole voice
              let the air in your lungs come out like a
phoenix soaring up from the ashes of
                    death) yell yell yell yell
      alleluia alleluia alle   alle   alle   LUUUUia

HE'S ALIVE

        shout it from the church towers from the
              clifftops from the
backs of eagles on the top of the sky on the top of
        the world make a joyful noise a
        noise of JOY of HOPE
                of LIFE!—!
                What a happy day
a day to make noises so great they echo around the whole
                    entire earth
        because no noise will be great enough to
        express the joy of
          the burn of our hearts within us
    alleluia alleluia all all all alle   alle   alle   alle
                    alleLUUUIA
                ALLELUIA THE JOY

HE'S ALIVE

look OUR SIN IS DEAD and OUR SHAME IS
DEAD and OUR

DEATH IS DEAD AND WILL BE NO MORE

sing
  sing
    sing
      sing
four-part no
   eight-part no
      sixteen-part harmonies
our sin is gone and we are white and clean sing
    SING to the One Who Is White
and Who has made us white like Him like a dove and
Whose Love Endures FOREVER
   (and ever and ever and ever because)

HE'S ALIVE

   and in Him we are restored from
  our ashes into the flames of His
   everlasting
    Life!

Bird's-Eye View

I've left toy towns behind me on the ground
Toy trees, toy cars.
I'm watching storms below me fall away
Beneath a cloud.
I hardly can believe this world I've found—
I'm in the stars—
For joy like this on such a normal day
Can't be allowed.

Jericho

I belong in Jericho,
the day on which it
fell:
I deserve to lose the life I never once used well.

I belong in Jericho—
anonymous
and dead.
      I should have watched the walls all fall
and turned,
with them,
bloodred.

I belong in Jericho:
it's just my just reward.
      But scarlet looks a lot like blood.
And I've
      a scarlet cord.

No More of Drowning

She'd lost herself
in pain, so when her head had breached the waves, she
    tried to find herself again—
though there was not much there but rain.
Her shoulders rose above the cold into
a different sort of world;
   she shivered, looked around her once,
   and shook her long-submergéd mane.
The sky above the surface was a sky she hadn't seen before.
It leaked still, grey and listless drops, much like
   the currents underneath;
   but there was light that bent in them, unlike
   the lightless place of pain,
     and something she'd not known beneath
came to her eyes amidst the rain:
    an arc
      of colors, pale, but
         there.

The colors seemed so fragile, bare,
   and yet they were the world; because in them
   she thought she glimpsed herself,
   a child no more of drowning, but of air.

She'd lost herself in pain,
    but when she saw
the open sky, she found a world she'd never known:
the womb released her from its own:
and she left
   the ocean-tomb where she had lain.

Awakening

April's warm blue breath
Thaws out muscles that were ice:
Streams can run again.

Even Me

I stutter
       and stammer
             and stumble
on speech,
and scoffing words scamper just
                  out of reach.

My tongue trips
       o
       v
       e
       r
       the easiest word:
my thoughts are all
                scattered—

yes, it's absurd—

but none of it matters.
God works either way.
And even if I
       have nothing to say,

yes, even without
easy
train
tracks
to ride,

       He chose even me:
even me!—
for His side.

Angels

The battleground is bloody,
And my coat is coming torn;
The other men are haggard:
Scarred and scared and sad and worn;

But I can see what they cannot,
The chariots of flame—
An army sure of victory,
That comes in God's own name:

Angelic—insufficient word
For those protecting me!
A legion clad in white and gold
As far as I can see!

A thousand men may fall beside,
But angels yet defend
My life and soul and footsteps—for,
Their Leader is my friend.

Harness

Let go and lean back:
the rope's got you,
the rope's got you
and all you need
to do is trust it.
The cliff face is
sheer, yeah,
but hey:
you've
got
a harness.

You could just freeze there and
bite your lip, but what's the
point in that? Dive in.
You've got a harness:
a God who will
never let
you fall.

You can let go of the rocks,
and it's okay.
The rocks won't hold you anyway.
Dive in.
Go ahead, dive in.
Let go and lean back
and He'll catch you,
because
when has He ever failed you before?

Lullaby

Do not fear the blade, my darling,
Do not fear the blade—
For though the steel stills the beating heart,
Though it can soul and body rend apart,
Your spirit in our God is staid,
So do not fear the blade.

Do not fear the night, my darling,
Do not fear the night—
For even in the terrors of the dark,
The Son has made his everlasting mark:
To Him the dark is as the light,
So do not fear the night.

Do not fear the pain, my darling,
Do not fear the pain—
Find comfort in the Hope of things ahead—
Your scars will be unscarred, because He bled!
Your Savior's wounds are not in vain,
So do not fear the pain.

Do not fear the end, my darling,
Do not fear the end—
For He who loved as we could never dream
Will wake us sleepers with His living stream;
The Lord of Time counts you His friend,
So there will be no end.

His Words, and Mine
Or, Unlikely Lucky Love. Or, Iambic Ice Skates.

his words, they
        skate
on sheets of crystal ice—
as agile and
        as smooth
        as gliding blades;
as glimmering as
        silver sweeping by,
they slide in gleaming scudding
        swift parades.

        my words, they
            jump
in tumbling jumbled thoughts,
        in syllables too mixed
        to understand,
in exclamation!
        points
and semi-
        hums:
and demi-colons
        never really planned.

his words, they
        float
like cirrus on the breeze;
like feathers or
        confetti thrown in streams,
the colored handfuls drifting
        to the ground,
but never touching earth:
        so many dreams.

i'm sure that shakespeare
                    never
presupposed
how my words,
                    they would
                                        jump
from his stress schemes:
they leave iambic
                    pentameter bars,
                    in thoughtless mangled bursts
of half-formed themes.

our words, they
            change
the way we used to think,
            communicate in
honey-tasting tones,
and show me
        what a lucky girl i am,
                    that even with my stuttered
                    mangled moans—

and even with his smooth
sweet baritones—

        he aids me when i crumple
        on the rink.

Hey

Hey, it's
been a week.

And streams once buried deep
have gained the bravery to speak:

and I can't quite describe how much a difference
it can make

to live a week, and only one.
To dig at springs, and slake.

Unimmured

Exposed from the walls of myself, my pride
Is undergoing suicide;
It's seeping out and setting free
The Me that I was made to be.

Sound into my Silence

Speak to me.
I simply want to hear your voice, the way it rolls
On languid wheels over
Broken, peaceful dusty roads;
It pulls the burden off my back in sweet forgetting loads.

Sing to me.
The melody that's loose and simple, drifting
Like a broken string, grey, wistful on the
Dreaming breeze;
It takes away my troubled cares with dandelion ease.

Stay with me.
I cannot trek the withered world
In courage everywhere alone,
I just can't stand the echoes
In my head: it's far too quiet:
A world of dry and silent men,
Of coffins, and of bone:
Please—speak to me,
And sing for me.
I love when you
Sound life
Where there is none.

Façade

My dear, my dear,
Come in,
Come in,
And see behind my walls:
If truly you possess the key,
Come wander in my halls,
And see the things I've hidden deep
Behind my clean façade;
View all my secret, hidden sins
And all the ways I'm flawed.

No one knows my heart except my
Lonely, outcast soul, and the God who,
When I ran from Him,
Came in to make me whole:
But with a mop and scarlet soap
He's washing dirt away,
And even when it's gone
He'll never leave me for a day.

So lover, if you dare to enter in
My hidden rooms,
Then find not crystal shining
But the filth of whited tombs—
And find, as well, the Savior
Who is scrubbing out the mud,
And find that any good in me
Was put there by His blood.

Kindred Spirit

You're like me.
It's great to know that someone else is
Just like me.
Like me
You're overrun with silly problems,
And you trip on fragile strands of love
In just the ways
I do.
A bit obsessed with what you want;
A bit depressed sometimes, you flaunt
Your carefree nonchalance
With such capricious little jaunts
That all the world is fully fooled.
Our lonely resources are pooled.
You don't know what it means to find that
You're like me.
But wait, you probably do; for
After all, I'm
Just like you.

Living Art

the venus de milo may not have as many arms as you have
but she's missing something else too
some color in her cheeks
some sparkle in her eyes
the life and vibrancy
i've always admired in you

and the mona lisa has
that mysterioso smile
but you have a smile that lights up
the cellar we live in
it's like the moon reflecting
the sun in your soul.

yeah it's a little rough getting through life
yeah the thief comes in and steals,
the paint cracks and gets chipped away
and the clay goes brittle and
we get old and we die,
but at the same time
you can live forever, you have the best Keeper
and he made you with a neverending soul.

so don't get too worried
you know
there's more beauty in you
more joy and eternity
than anyone will find in transient
brush marks.

Your Eyes

They say blue eyes
are like the sea:
as deep
as bright
as free.

And brown eyes, warm and dark—
liquid chocolate
hits
the mark.

Grey eyes, stormy,
m e s m e r i z i n g,
green eyes, bright and so s u r -

                             p r i s i n g,

purple, high as haughty jewels,
ensnaring wiser men
and fools.

But your eyes,
call them what they please,
are treasure holds—and mine,
the keys
to open up your chest of laughs
and s l o o o o w
oncoming epitaphs—
your eyes are full of
joy, of
love,
of glimpses
of the world above;

no seas or chocolate pools for me,
no high enthroned prosperity,
for when I followed
where you walked,
in vaults of joy
you had me—

locked.

He Sings with Grace

The rhythms are a part of me:
the sync   opated beats, the sea
of surging meters, bars in waves—
they flood my hidden seaside caves.

I'm an island; melodies
(when measured, deeper than my knees)
are oceans surging up the beach
and flowing through my longing reach.

Salt leaves stains on sandy shores,
feet leave prints on dusty floors,
music leaves its surging trace
behind it on my island's face.

The music is a part of me,
a washing through of song and sea
and surging, surging, surging tide:
it cleanses me from the inside.

Journeying Jointly

Two voices can become a single voice:
One, roaring and glittering, and one
That whispers matte, can both come to rejoice
As one, and blend into a single run;
Two songs can pour their ardour in one praise,
Two melodies with different qualities
Can shine as one, though going separate ways,
One single brilliance from two harmonies;
And, so, two souls can take two different roads,
And step to different rhythms on their way,
And bear two very different sorts of loads,
With different hopes and different things to pray:
       But in their different travels, trials and strife,
       Two souls can be as one in One Man's life.

The Church

A Whole is made of hearts:
                              one thousand beating parts
                    in single time
            can all be one, and have
one reason
            and
                  one rhyme.

A Whole is made of parts:
            of frac-
                        tures, frag
                                    -ments, bits of wood
        and some of plastic and
                of stone
                and some of bad and some
of good.

A Whole is made of wood
            the way a family is a tree, and
            all the bits of stone and branches see
they
        need
                a River   to
                                        be
                                                good.

A Whole is full and good,
            with Water quenching all its parts—
                the trunk
                into the branches' wood.

For blood must feed our hearts.

IV

the exile

Oops

He freed me from my shackles—
gave me friends, a home, a break—
He showed a Love so wonderful I handed Him a stake:
not minding if He tied me; either way, I'd never go!

And then I ran away again. Before I told Him so.

A Letter to a...Love

You've been waiting;
let's pretend this epistle is
Me.

You can now dub me dauntless,
for I, in person,
have conquered all my fears
and come to reclaim an old—
shall we say friend?
It is good to see you again.
Delightful, in fact, for you are looking
Quite Well.
I would comment on your newly-cut hair
or the inch and a half I've not seen on you before,
but I do believe the sun's in my eyes.
Fancy that. And
just at the wrong moment, too.

I digress. Shall we surpass formalities
and get on with it, perchance?
I have come to apologize.
As you wished.
In person.
What, can you not see how I entreat you,
on one humble knee?
My right hand is resting on your forearm,
as it has done so many times before,
the way we missed it doing.
(It is so very good to see you again.)
I am sincere, truly.

I suppose the only flaw in this meeting
is that you're so very quiet.
I can't read your mind, you know—
Darling.
Speak back.
I long to hear your voice again, your dulcet,
honest tones, the way you roll your r's
into undeserved compliments:
I suppose I need them to
heighten my hellish self-esteem. But—
well, the sun is in my eyes.
Are you angry, dear?
Are you angry at the invisible,
intangible and utterly imaginary
hand on your beautiful arm?
I am too.
I am only afraid I cannot do any better,
for now.
I send—
No, I say aloud—
Much Love.

Please.
Forgive me.

You Asked My Advice?

The most powerful position I will ever have
is friend.

To be a rock—why, my bones aren't hard enough for that,
my mind not solid enough,
and yet I must try or
she will fall—

a word of advice
can send an eagle's nest—
plummeting—

Hyp. Ocrite.

I
am such
a hyp
-ocrite
I
give advice & don't
follow
it
I
honestly
am trying,
but
to live a theory's
to break a rut.

Clock

As punctual as a clock,
I tick
tick
tock:
each tick the same iniquity,
each tock the same remorse.

My hour hand
will circumscribe my numbered list of sins,
no slave to serendipity
(Time always, always wins)—
and battering the Ten Commandments—
shattering the Two, will mangle every rule it hits,
and every other too.

A hundred days—
a thousand—
no, a million cycling by—
I cannot count the sins I've sinned,
no matter how I try.

My second hand
won't falter as it jumps around
your face;
but will seduce me deep into
some Godforsaken place.

And when I have emerged,
as I am always wont to do,
I'll grieve my broken state and all the
broken tablets,
too.

Fleshly

I don't know how it's possible to leave a God like You—
A God of color, majesty and grace—and yet I do.

The breath you breathed on me is now
    a facet of my lungs,
      but when I speak I try to speak alone
        without your tongues.
The blood you spilled to write your love to me
    is in my veins;
      and yet my pen writes only in
        my own dull stains.

O God, who gave me red and blue
    and blood and air
      and heartbeat, You
   have rent the brimming grave asunder!
     And even still!
          I always wander.

Word-Weary

Reading is hard.
You are given a dense stack of papers
with hard white edges and blotted
black ink crowding the meticulous space,
and you are expected to extract from it
a world
of green and gold.

My laptop screen is
looking is
easy.
You know,
if the colors are already in your throat,
there is no need to masticate them.

It would be nice if the most important things in life
were more generally the
looking sort.

But alas.
God gave us
a book.

The Line and the Pit

Every step I take is
                              stepping wrong.
The   tightrope of my hope   is quick   to sway
                    in every wind,
                                        so as I go along
I trip and
            fall and
            stumb-
                    ling, lose the way.

I love Your law, but
                              how I hate it too—
it saves me and I leave it, *every day,*
                    for something that is
                                        lesser, pale, untrue—
                    I love the lesser things—
                                        they take me prey—
I'm captive to the pit beneath the line;
                    I try to keep my footing, yet I slay
                              my best affections—and I
                                                    fall
                                                    from
                              Thine:
O Lord,
a thousand times
I lose   the way.

If I'm to reach the far side of the pit,—

                              I'll need Your wings
                                        to fly me over it.

Christmas Ho-Hum

The lamb in the stable
must have seen the baby and wondered
how that small brown crying thing
could die in blood-payment for the entire world,
how it could be
the One Lamb.

The shepherds in the swards
must have heard the mighty host with disbelief
because the Lord of the Universe meant to use
the same sort of helpless
farm animal they'd been tending
as the Shepherd of their own souls.

The stars in the sky
must have seen their newest counterpart
with bewilderment and joy, because
That Star
hailed the Bringer of All Light,
a small brown crying thing
in a stable
in a nowhere-town
in a little country
on a tiny earth.

The people in the suburban streets
see this scene in faded plastic figurines and think, *cute,*
and go on with their shopping.

Here

I could have been born
across the world
in a bombed and shaking sphere.
Instead, I'm an American
and I've
no fear.

I could have been one of
the lowest caste
and known only pagan gods.
Instead, I'm rich in God and goods
against
all odds.

I could have been
orphaned, slaved or starved—
all three, and more beside;
I could have lost
my loves, my home—
to hell, I could have died—
and yet I wasn't
didn't
don't.
I live in luxury.

And God, I thank you every day,
but wonder,
why
me?

Unremembering

Whirl me around,
Just like you did the other day
When times were easy.
Dip me to the ground,
And think of all the things we did that
They called cheesy.
I simply want to unremember
Everything that happened after that:
I miss, I miss our love before the spat.
So spin me, dearest,
Spin me in a cyclone,
So fast that neither one of us can think.
And then we'll stay afloat
Upon the bog of memory,
Please dip me, so we never ever sink.

Lonesome

I missed this, I missed
        you,—(I missed it all)—
                to sit and talk and know I have a friend:
       I missed the way you lean against the wall so cozy,
                  lingering long there past the end;
I missed the way we feel,
      just the same
                    as one another, twins in every way;
       I missed the way you laugh
       into my name,
               a tender trill upon the note you play.
See, most of all I missed
      your love for me;
            you show it as a sister, ceaseless, kind
                 and never breaking off; abundantly
you show me that I'm on your heart and mind.

Could sisters dwell together—time could freeze—
if only you didn't have to leave—stay, please?

Finity

For a boy I never knew

O Lord i—
why?
he had a life to live,
he had a family, a home—
he was healthy (i presume,
he was in sports i know)—
he wasn't supposed to—
why?
he had classes, finals are next week,
he could have graduated sometime—
but i don't know him, i don't know
when that would have been—
and then the accident happened
(some accident, i don't even know what)
and the track meet i guess just ended and—
he was an american college kid with
so much ahead of him, God,
he would have had so much ahead of him.
maybe i'm just in shock because
it could have happened to me;
because even at a white school in a rich neighborhood
life is frail and finite and
we don't have the control we think we have.
but God, this was never supposed to happen—
why, why does it happen—
he wasn't supposed to
die.

At...Rest?

You sit silently, for
there is nothing you can say.

Empty words
of hopeless hope,
reassured of nothing.
Rope makes such a stifling noose,
to let the words fall free and loose
you'd have to burn the bonds away.
But grief won't let the fire light:
too wet and red and quenching
like the night.

So nothing comes to bring a ray
of hope
or faith
or right.

There's nothing you can say.

Confused

Is it a time to laugh or cry?
Rejoice, or mourn a life gone by?
To speak, or cry a silent rain,
Remember, or forget the pain
Of someone we had known and lost?
Why do we pay this priceless cost?
For things are Different now, you know,
They're different everywhere we go.
We cannot act the same again.
So laugh, or cry? And then—what then?

Cramped

The time—why were we made to have so small
A length of time packed (wrinkled, too) in this,
Our withered iron cage of cramped-up life—

And why—why can I not just sing through all,
And live a lily's life of carelessness—
Instead I'm locked in iron and know strife!

God help me!—I'm a claustrophobic louse, I fall
And have no patience—none, nor faith—in this
Your plan for me, your plan—eternal life?

Rahab

I'm lowly, Lord;
a sinner in a craven city,
keening for my life
and for my family,
for because you are just
we are doomed.

Yet a God of justice
must have mercy too,
mustn't he?
Will he have mercy
on lowly me?

A red cord in the window,
or lamb's blood on the door:
I trust that you will save me, for
I'm lowly, Lord.
I've nothing but a hope from You.
I pray it's true.

Finals
Wheaton College, May 2017

We're packing up,
looking at the boxes in people's doorways as they rise
from the ground
smelling cleaning chemicals from every room
filtering out mentally the white noise of the vacuum
wondering what it means that this floor
will never be quite this same floor again.

There was so much buildup to this but it came
so fast: Easter, wild sadness and joy at the
salvation we have from our Savior's death
and then Saturday a tragedy happened and
a boy I never knew became one I could never meet,
and here we are packing
the boxes piling higher
the rooms losing their personalities and
gaining their initial sterility
and *our* floor
resets to be
a floor
again.

Goodbyes, goodbyes,
frantic hugs and hectic finals
we study so much and clean so much it seems like
everything is slipping away and we don't
have time to hold on to it,
to take deep breaths from the air of this year
(though if we did all we'd smell is Windex anyway);
and the hands that stopped
two months ago on the clock in the bathroom

stand still, although our hands are too
busy for us to think about them,
although time circles around and around and comes
back to where it started every twelve hours,
and even so moves forward and *won't* stop.

Outside the trees are in bloom, dressed for a regalia
or a wedding, celebrating the year we had?
Or the fact that it is over?
Are they ushering in the new freshman who will
give our rooms colors again, are they hailing
the next twelve hours that begin as ours end,
are they simply glad to see us go?
Perhaps we'll never know.
Though one boy from the other dormitory
might already know.

The trees become married while this boy is buried;
boxes are filled and shelves are swept and
mirrors wiped of the stains we
scattered across them through the year,
and meanwhile a coffin is lowered into the ground and
flower petals spiral on the winds and
the palm fronds we got three Sundays back slowly
turn brown and crisp on the floors where we threw them
and everything is at the same time returning
to a place it's been before.
Life cycles. It grows and fades, it rises and falls,
but mostly right now it seems
it falls.

And here we are, packing up.
With no time
to process.

V

the new earth

Wishness

It's that bit of stillness
        we wish we could touch, the
                not-quite-something of Life or of Death
    that we cannot iron onto paper—
the hope of love and the love of hope, and
the fear of death and the death of fear and
      the silent grey skies arching in brimming barrenness
        and whispering through the paper wind chimes
            of autumn trees—
it's That bit of stillness
        that leaves us returning to the stale words like
        heartbeat and depths of soul,
     nostalgia, loss, emotion,
          profundities of words ironed
          as flat as they can be, to try and
          transport them to other lives,
              when really all they can do is bring back
what lives inside each one's Own stomach,
               the hunger
        for something
    unslakable
    on earth.

The Only Way

You know, I get it, life doesn't always make sense.

I hate
how none of the little boxes we create
seems to fit this life all the time,
how the idea that we are made like God contradicts
all the actions of every dictator ever,
how the hope of things to come often
pales in comparison to the present heartache of
life on earth.

I plead with God
because sometimes I wonder how a
Being whose name is Love
can let His children stab each other with knives
and shoot with guns, how such a Being can
be okay with tsunamis that destroy whole villages
and watch as His creatures one by one go extinct.

I can't prove
that God exists, any more than I can turn back
time a billion years
and watch for signs of macroevolution, so sometimes
I wonder if He's even there.
Sometimes I get awfully close to deciding He's not.

I get it. I hate it. I cry.

And I stick with this crazy religion anyway.

Because if there is no God, I have
no purpose living.
If there is no hope, I have
no reason to keep slogging through concrete.
If there is no eternity,
then my brief eighty years of existence
is shit.
Pardon the language.
But without God I am
absolutely nothing, I am the tiny red mite
squashed accidentally under life's shoe.

So, yeah. I get it. I get
why you hate believing in God.
But for me, anyway,
I keep coming back, because
I see no alternative.

Early-Morning Truth

Someday it will all make sense.
I envy the time when Truth
will come out of her tents,
blinking in the early-morning sunlight
and wetting her feet in
the dew, and things that are True
will be seen
for what they are:

each, a
tree or tent or camping maiden,
not the cloudy mirrors that pretend
to be windows or the medals
that shine with pyrite luster
or the vixen whose heart
is not involved in her flirtation.

Truth will be evident,
still in her woolen pajamas,
and will fix coffee over an open fire.

I don't know when we'll get there, but
I trust that we will.
We know she's in her tent.
It's just a matter of
coaxing her out
so we can look her in the eyes.

Heaven's Portal

The grass glows green from the recent rain;
the rest of the world, swollen shades of grey;
cool sky on the skin of our arms swaddles
cries of birds that beckon in the twilight,
that leave behind echoes
of plaintive joy—

You can feel spring through the cracked windows,
as one reads heaven through cracked pages of earth.

Soft

Soft and strange and sudden
         is the morning,
                  quiet, clear and
empty of the past.
         Trials vanish into mists for
                  every heart knows
                           nothing earthly ever dares to last.

Hard and too familiar
is the daylight, and
hardships, once
the scent of night descends,
will never give us peace until
the morning, when all the graphic suffering
         fades and ends.

Unremembered trials
leave us aching,
         but someday they will
                  soften in the mists.
Unremembered scars
made in the gloaming
         will someday be obscured
                  from aching wrists.

Soft and strange and sudden
         is the morning,
                  gauzy like a veil of falling snow.
Though you and I and every heart
has felt the bitter wind,
                  the morning always comes again,
                           we know.

Cinders

When everything's taken,
it hurts.
You know as well as I that
it hurts.

Close your eyes, and hope,
and someday you'll be restored.
Close your heart, and cherish
what you had, and your reward
will come;
but for now it hurts.

It's all right if your fist clenches
and your knuckles stand out as
snow-capped mountains along your hand;
the bone might show through
but it's all right, because
your heart does not.

When every dream's shaken,
it hurts.
But hold on; you have a new one cradled
in your white-knuckled hand.

I've Grown

I've grown, you know. I'm different now.
I see things in a different way.
And though I can't take back the things I
always used to think and say,
they just don't matter anymore—
I'm washed of what is old.
The Sea has cleared my prints away,
and newness, so I'm told,
is total when it's from the Sea.
In fact I show no single mark of what I used to be,
so watch—I'll make you new marks, straighter,
bolder than before.
I've grown, you know. I'm something less
and something much, much more.

There's More of Me

I am not a creature of this earth.
I know, for if I were,
I'd never long for other worlds
Beyond the scope of human eyes
And ears
And tastes
And thoughts
And fears
And earthly lies.

I am not the daughter of the dark.
I know, for if I were,
I'd never lie asleep at night
And dream of stars and moons and light
And life
And joy
And peace
And hope
And truer sight.

I am more than merely flesh and blood.
I know, behind the workings of my heart—
Behind the mechanism
That is pumping
In my chest,
Are love and hate—
A soul
With deep unrest.

You may disregard my tangled thoughts.
I know, for some say science
Is the only thing around;
But faith, I know, is real too,
And when
My heart
Pours out its soul,
I trust
It's firm and true.

Dig up Your Box and Ditch It, Please.

Christianity is not
goody-two-shoe white girls preaching kumbaya with Bibles
the destruction of native cultures by an unnatural religion
crude misogynistic womanization
or scientific ignorance.

Christianity is not
campfire ditties and side hugs because
its leader came specifically with
a sword,
and it is not
old-fashioned femininity or uppity white supremacy
because this leader was gentle and submissive and so on
but He
was a Middle Eastern Man.

Christianity is not
the crumbler of native tribal
infrastructures because it belongs to
all peoples and tribes and nations and gives to Caesar
what is Caesar's, requiring no giving up of cultural heritage
(unless you count the universal human desire for Hell
as heritage).

Christianity is not
men taking advantage of women or preventing them from
reaching their full potential because Jesus
cursed the Pharisees yet would not stone the adulteress
and we know there is no
Jew Greek slave free man *or* woman in Him
at all, but all are
one.

Christianity is not
mindless reasonless foolish
deranged unhinged outdated
or mutually exclusive of scientific fact because
we simply believe it was God who made
gravity, soundwaves, electrons and heartbeats
rather than
what do you believe made those things again?
themselves?

Please rid yourself of these stereotypes,
it is not because of these that
I marvel fully at objective marvelousness
and celebrate art as an emulance of God's own soul
and strive to love as a Middle Eastern Man did
and dig through my heart-vomit with a shovel to do so
and feast monthly on flesh and blood.

Christianity is not a corpse
in a box.

Faith Is

She didn't know

       that the stairs would hold her, but

          they were made of stone

             so she climbed them anyway.

Faith Is Not

it's a sixty foot

drop but science is
stupid you know i'ma ju

mp

Death First, Then Life

If you wish to live, you have to die.
A paradox, it's true; but tell me now how caterpillars
weave dark coffins for themselves
and climb inside
before they learn to fly?

Wouldja Look at That

Credibility
is hard to come by, but when
you see with your own eyes the law in action
that accords with the principle you already
knew,
when the broken-in sandals are
just what you have heard they ought to feel like
after the blisters
and you find that exercise does, in fact,
make you healthier,
when you bear a child and the baby is really
alive—
why,
principles can be tested after all.

Labyrinth

Life| maze   that   you }
| is a / .rehpiced ot evah

Complications abound.
So does pain.

You'll never} / want to
  {dnif yllaer/   you / go.
  your way where/

It's hard that way.
But God's got your back.
He'll give you a string like Ariadne's
(His Word)
To guide you, and even if }
{ ,tsol elttil a teg uoy
He'll show you the
              / Right /
              / Way   /
              / Again./

Trust Him.
He's got your }
  .kcab

Safe

The sky is dark
and from its stark
and looming cloud
streams rain.

The streetlamps stare,
through frigid air
and down our shadowed lane.

But inside, in
the yellow house,
The thunder doesn't roar.
And safe behind
the windowpanes,
we laugh at lightning; for,
we're wrapped in tranquil arms:
the house's comforting embrace:

there's nothing that can hurt us
when we're sheltered in God's grace.

Prison Break

Now in Time's unbroken walls
We wake and live and die;
But when the prison, shattered, falls,
We'll bid our years goodbye.

      Forever
Will take meanings new—
Our everlasting hope,   break through,
And weak forevers bound in chain
             Will wrench their bodies free again—
         On, eternal music roll!
         Bells rejoice with every toll!
            Follow, now, the trumpet's pull!
      And all will dance;
And sleep, perchance,
      Will dream in fear no more.

             For home again we'll be
             When we from Time are free.

But now—as Time's prevailing walls
Surround us for the night—
We'll wait until our Savior calls
And breaks   us into light.

Jordan's Stormy Banks

Do you see it?
On the other side, the land
we've heard so much about?
I hear there are rivers of living water,
water which if you sip it once will heal you forever—
water to wet the parchedness in your throat,
cool water so sweet it softens the soreness all through
a tired body, water that flows endlessly
and eternally and never runs out.
And we can drink it, soon.

Do you see it?
The way the grass and flowers glow, a plush carpet
in a luscious paradise, I can almost feel them
under my aching feet!
Though right now on this side
my bare skin bleeds from the rocks.
Look, you could sleep like a king, right there
on the ground in that grass:
a royal bed of ambrosial perfumes.
And we can rest there, soon.

Do you see it?
There's no sun over there, because the King
shines with such brilliance that
even on this side His light feels good
on my cold, gooseflesh arms.
And what must it be like
to be there, wrapped all around in His arms?
And we can run to them, soon!

My throat is so dry—
my feet are so worn—
I haven't really rested in
all my many years,
but feeling that light,
smelling the grass and the breeze and the
flowers that bloom so wildly on the other shore—

do you see it? Do you see it,
tell me do you see it?
My body feels more awake,
just seeing it!—

For I know that
we can live there, soon.

Further Reading

Scripture

You can't fully slake your thirst until you've read from the Living Word. This book is an introduction to, or at most a pulling-together of, the Christian Scriptures; it is not a substitute for them. If you wish to continue the journey begun here, you must go back to its beginning, to the Word itself. My suggestion is to start with the Gospels and Psalms using Crossway's English Standard Version® (ESV®), a readable and accurate translation.

The Gospels. Matthew, Mark, Luke and John all tell the same story of a Man, the Son of God and at the same time One with God, who came to live and die with the human race to save it because He loved it. These are the heart of the Bible. They are the culmination of every hope in the Old Testament and the basis for all of salvation in the New.

The Psalms. The rawness and honesty of the Psalms, and the concreteness and physicality of their imagery, have been praised for millenia as great poetry—even by those who do not believe in the God they describe. The Psalms do not always have answers to their questions, but they are not scared to mourn over the injustice of the world. Much if not all of my work draws from their ideas and images.

Understanding the Bible

Historical context, scientific theory, and modern-day applications of the Bible are all helpful in understanding the Christian faith—for non-Christians, but equally for Christians. Below are works that have changed my way of understanding the Bible and Christianity.

Pearcey, Nancy. *Total Truth*. Crossway, 2008.
This book is what convinced me that Christianity is true. Modern culture tends to act as if science and religion are entirely separate entities, but Pearcey shows that for a worldview to make sense it must incorporate both these things into one wholistic explanation of ultimate reality.

Richter, Sandra. *The Epic of Eden*. InterVarsity, 2008.
This book is a very readable and helpful explanation of how the events of the Old Testament fit into the salvation of the New.

The Westminster Confession of Faith. Center for Reformed Theology and Apologetics, 2016, www.reformed.org /documents/wcf_with_proofs/index.html. Accessed 1 Jul. 2017.
The Westminster Confession works systematically through the main ideas of the Christian and specifically the Reformed faith to show what we believe and why we believe it. This website also has links to detailed Scripture proofs.

Literature and Poetry

I would not be the author I am without the thoughts and images and sounds of the poets of the past, from Dickinson to Shakespeare to Homer to the Psalmists.

Alter, Robert. *The Book of Psalms*. W. W. Norton, 2007.

Dickinson, Emily. *The Complete Poems of Emily Dickinson*. Edited by Thomas H. Johnson, Back Bay, 1960.

Hollens, Peter. "Poor Wayfaring Stranger." *Hollens*, feat. the Swingle Singers, independent record, 2012, https://www.youtube.com/watch?v=GaJ3adMgsbY

Homer. *The Odyssey*. Translated by Robert Fagles, Penguin, 1997.

Shakespeare, William. *Hamlet*. Edited by G. R. Hibbard, Oxford, 2008.

Shakespeare, William. *Shakespeare: The Poems*. Edited by David Bevington, Bantam, 1988.

Stennett, Samuel. "On Jordan's Stormy Banks." *Indelible Grace Hymnbook*, music by Christopher Miner, 1997.

Trinity Hymnal: Revised Edition. Twelfth printing, Great Commission Publications, 2004.

Margaret J. Rothrock is a writing major at Wheaton College, IL, though she spends the rest of her time in Central Pennsylvania with her family, her lapdog, and her increasingly large number of books. She won two national medals in the 2016 Scholastic Art and Writing Awards for her poems. You can find her at www.keysandthings.blog.

Made in the USA
San Bernardino, CA
23 July 2017